The Mazemaker's Daughters

For Lesley

from

Angela Stoner

Angie

Oversteps Books

First published in 2016 by   Oversteps Books Ltd
6 Halwell House
South Pool
Nr Kingsbridge
Devon
TQ7 2RX
UK

www.overstepsbooks.com

Printed in Great Britain by imprint digital, Devon.

This book is dedicated to Dorothy Coventon
with love and thanks

Acknowledgements

With grateful thanks to Zeeba Ansari, who was painstaking in her help with early poems and invaluable in helping me find the Minotaur's voice.
Thanks to fellow poets, Martha Street, Verity Schanche and Jenny Hamlett.
Thanks to Penelope Shuttle, who first helped shape the piece from a shadowy idea.
Thanks to Alice Taylor for tutoring and mentoring me through the process. Both were tutors for The Poetry School.
Thanks to Katrina Naomi for close study of several poems.
Thanks to Penzance Stanza group, in particular Lesley Hale, Mary Oliver and Christine Curtis.
Thanks to The Poetry School and The Poetry Society.
Thanks to John Morey for help with proof-reading and technical problems.

This collection was conceived as a whole, so very few poems have been sent in to magazines or competitions, but versions of some poems have appeared in *Acumen* and *Loose Muse*, and some sections performed at festivals.

Contents

Foreword

Deep below the palace of Knossos, in an impenetrable labyrinth, lives a minotaur, a monster who is half-man and half-beast. The miserable creature was born to the Queen of Crete, Pasiphaë, as a way to punish the over-reaching, god-defying pride of her husband. This powerful myth reverberates in our psyche with a multi-layered and disturbing resonance. There is a cast of larger-than-life actors in this story: Minos the arrogant king who dared to think he could outwit and even command the gods; Pasiphaë his wife, who was cursed into lusting after a bull; her daughter Ariadne who fell in love with an enemy of Crete and ended up causing the death of her half-brother, the Minotaur. The Minotaur himself — a tortured soul, neither man nor beast — is unforgettable. Then there is the intriguing builder and designer of the labyrinth himself, Daedalus, possesed of endless powers of invention and craftsmanship.

Daedalus is recorded as having a son, the famous Icarus, but nowhere are daughters mentioned. However, when you wander in the labyrinth of the psyche, you can't always account for what you find. As Sir Arthur Evans, the archaeologist wrote: *everything around ... the dark passages ... would conspire to produce a sense of the supernatural. It was haunted ground, and then, as now, 'phantasms' were about.*

(MacGillivray, p. 194)

The first time I wandered in the labyrinth of my imagination, the daughters were there, only whispers at first, glimpsed as shadows or phantasms just seen out of the corner of the eye. But as I continued with my exploration they became very clear and their voices insistent. So I have given Daedalus, the mazemaker, daughters. And who is to say he had no daughters? In many versions of the myth he is a slave of Minos, and it is unlikely that the daughters of a slave would get any mention in history. They have demanded that I place them in the centre of this work, and so I have.

The myth of the Minotaur, and Who's Who in *The Mazemaker's Daughters*

There are many versions of the myth, but most agree on the following basic facts.

Minos, the king of Crete, begged **Poseidon**, the god of the sea, to give him a bull worthy of sacrifice to a god. The bull so surpassed any in his herd that Minos contrived to keep the beast, and began boasting that he could command the gods.

To punish him for his arrogance, Poscidon caused **Pasiphaë**, the Queen of Crete, to become enamoured of the bull and to give birth to a hideous monster, **the Minotaur**, who was half-bull and half-man.

Daedalus, a master craftsman and inventor, was at the court of King Minos, and in some versions is a slave of the king. Among his inventions was a dance floor for **Ariadne**, one of the many daughters of King Minos. When Queen Pasiphaë fell in love with the bull, Daedalus devised a wooden cow in which she could hide. Daedalus later constructed the labyrinth in which the Minotaur was confined. Once a year, young men and maidens were thrown into the labyrinth to be devoured by the Minotaur.

Ariadne fell in love with one of these young men, **Theseus**, and helped him, with the gift of a magical thread and a sword, to find his way to the Minotaur and slay him.

The Daughters of Daedalus are not mentioned anywhere. He had a son, Icarus; and Daedalus created the wings with which they both attempted to fly. The daughters, **The Mazemaker's Daughters** of the title, are my invention.

Section One

Prologue

Come In

(i)

Dare you follow us into the labyrinth
where the Minotaur howls through millennia?

Can you resist the story?
Royal scandal. Royal baby.
Sex, bestiality.
A child imprisoned in a monster;
dismembered limbs and flesh
putrifying in an underworld.

Here! Take hold of the thread.
Feel it tug the way the moon tugs oceans.
If you take it, don't let go.
Fasten it tight to the outside world.

Lower your head if you dare and creep into the murk.

(ii)

You don't have to enter by the labyrinth.
There are many ways into any story.
Perhaps you'd prefer to enter
through the Palace of Knossos.

We can sit you on silk,
feed you pomegranates, figs and olives,
beef and cheeses to shock your tongue awake.

We'll pour you wine from crafted goblets
while you gaze at long-limbed girls and glowing frescoes,
wonder at all the wrought gold ornaments.

Enjoy the spectacle of bull-leaping.
Did you ever see such beasts, such athletes?

Listen to the minstrel's song.

Listen as the notes plunge.

The Mazemaker

Perhaps we could introduce you to the masterbuilder
Daedalus the slave, who'll build the maze,
the famous labyrinth that none can escape.

He made this glittering dance floor.
He built it for Ariadne, the favourite princess,
the one who's tipped to rule when Minos goes.

Daedalus has built walking, talking people,
ingenious thief-proof jewellery caskets.
He loves inventing – has a genius for puzzles.

He'll make the labyrinth and later fashion
wings for Icarus our brother.
We are his daughters.

We're never mentioned in any of the myths.
You'll never come across the tiniest footnote.

The Mazemaker's Daughters in the Palace

Our hands are never beaten and we never scrub with lye.
Our hands are soft enough to bathe a princess,
brush her hair and fold her silks.

Other slaves shiver in rags, are starved, are bruised.
We taste Ariadne's food,
wear her cast-off jewellery and clothes.

We're allowed to touch the Cattle of Crete,
to coax their udders into giving milk.
We've tasted its meadow pungency.

We hold our heads up high as any lady of the court
though no one ever curtsies to us
or knows our names.

Section Two

The White Bull from the Sea

The Dolls of Daedalus

Everyone gasps at such exquisite miracles,
life-sized men who walk and talk and do her bidding.
Our dad, you see, makes perfect dolls for Ariadne.

He gives us the ones which aren't quite perfect –
perhaps his fingers slipped a little, or the voice is just off-key.
They're still miraculous – designed for princesses not slaves.

In daylight hours we keep them locked away.
We only dare to play with them at night in hidden corners,
but how we love our armies of imperfect men!

We give them irreverent nicknames, make them bow to us.
After a day of being slapped and teased by Ariadne,
how wonderful to torment in our turn.

The men feel nothing. They are made of wood,
but crafted so cunningly they seem alive –
telling us constantly how much they love us.

In dusty and neglected corridors of the palace
we dance as quietly as gossamer
with our beautiful partners.

The Bull-Leaping

The sun beats down.
All eyes are on Ariadne
the favoured one, the sun princess.
We are her slave girls and we hold our heads up high.

The crowd sees we are dressed in gold and purple silk
and flank the sun princess.
None can see the mends in our robes,
their fraying edges or worn patches.

Drums beat. Choirs sing.
Flutes, harps and trumpets play.
Music soars to Olympus.

King Minos. Queen Pasiphaë.
Our rulers stand like gods above the hordes.
Flamed by sun, they shine with power.
King Minos thunders: *let the games begin.*

Magnificent specimens swagger out.
The envy of the world, our bulls and young men
creating a hammering in your chest
as though a drumskin would burst open.

The tournament goes on until the evening sun
paints Minos red as blood. He cries:
Poseidon, Ruler of the Sea
even the master of our herd
cannot be worthy of you.

Grant us a favour.
Send us a bull from the sea
worth sacrificing to a god.

Silence.

A bolt of fire.
Sky and ocean rear up.
Towering floods thunder down.

Riding mountains of water –
a massive pure white bull!

Pasiphaë Speaks to The Bull From The Sea

You emerged, as promised, from the sea –
white as its foam – mighty as its thunder.
Gleaming flanks – muscled neck.
Whole worlds revealed in your eyes.

Nuzzled against your skin where stench of earth
mingles with ocean's salty breath,
my fingers measure your whiteness.
Poseidon demands your death.

If you could mate before you die
divinely sire our Cretan herd,
make champion bulls that men can leap
for wealth, renown and Minos.

Any of our herd that you might serve
would be the Queen. Her offspring
would be a miracle, a legend in the world.
Crete would overflow with rich full cream.

You cannot stay. Oh pure white bull,
we must return you to the sea.

How Did He Dare?

Nobody dares say anything out loud but whispers rustle through the meadows
boasts from the king about ruling the sea, ruling the god of the sea.
A stupid switched sacrifice and the white bull from the ocean
still in Knossos, as if the king could fool Poseidon Shh!
This silence is unquiet, tastes more dangerous
than a raging tempest or a thunderbolt.
No good can come from this evil.
The vengeance will be terrible.
We know. We all know.
We say nothing.
Wait.

Backstairs Gossip

It's a secret plaything for the queen, he said,
like the dolls I used to make for Ariadne.

Daedalus must think we're blind and deaf and stupid.
In his head we must be six years old, still playing with his dolls.
Does he take us for fools?

He's such a favourite of the queen's,
more like a pet or courtier
no honest slave.

Doesn't he hear the whispers, the backstairs gossip
relishing the story of just what he's building and just what it's for?

A giant wooden cow
smelling and feeling like flesh and blood
designed to stir the lust of the white bull from the sea!

We know exactly how the queen intends to play –
exactly what she'll do inside that foul contraption:
spreading herself wide open on all fours
presenting herself like the filthy cow she is.

No matter how red and raw our hands
scrubbing graffiti from the palace walls,
no matter how pristine those walls appear each morning
the stench of her shame seeps into every stone.

The Queen Forgets Herself

His firm young flanks,
lust-damp eyes
animal magnetism!

Who can doubt
the divinity inhabiting
that pure white body?

Hard muscle, thrilling to my touch,
smooth skin an oily rich
incitement to embrace.

His appetite matching my wildest
fantasy. I long to grab his horns,
dance the bull-dance, naked.

His passion tears my womb.
My screams are all
bloodied ecstasy.

Ariadne Speaks

My mother's power is tainted.

It's common knowledge she's no longer seen as queen.
    Her command to spare my brother, seal his fate,
        must be her last edict.

My father's becoming a tyrant.
      I was born to be queen, give commands.
          He has stopped schooling me, begun to say
            men are natural leaders.

I am still young enough for now
      to slip into the shadow world of slaves. There
         under the guise of stealing sweetbreads
           I filch tittle-tattle.

For a while longer I can twist Minos
      round my little finger,
         wheedling the magic sword
           that should have been my birthright.

I sit with my grandmother
      winding wool and learning ancient arts.
         I'll spin an enchanted thread
           from the bloody cord binding
              my mother and her monster-son.

Now I alone can slip in and out
      between our world and the world
         of the labyrinth.

           I'm forced to muster different powers ...

Pasiphaë Considers the Imminent Birth

(i)

I'll never survive it.
My belly is bruised past bearing.
No midwife will survive it.
Minos will never let them live to tell the tale.
Even severed tongues wag.

(ii)

My poor offspring won't survive it.
Somebody must realise the kindness
in killing the miserable monster.
This imminent birth trails death behind it.
The aftermath will be a slaughterhouse.

(iii)

I declare my intentions, to my husband, the king:
Minos, I will bear this birth alone
The shame is mine and mine alone.

(iv)

I attempt a queenly carriage.
The monster inside me kicks so violently
I fall on all fours, bellowing.

(v)

I am rank with fear and pain
my hair all tumbled down.
Ariadne won't come near me these days
to plait and pin it as she used to.

(vi)

I taste the disgust in my husband's voice:
Woman, I have made the necessary arrangements.

Ariadne Watches the Birth of the Minotaur

My mother is a slut.
All the palace knows it
though none dare say so openly.
I will not blush for her.
I'll never plait her hair again.

I watch the birth.
At such moments, a queen becomes
like any other woman.
If anything she displayed less dignity
than any country wife.
The whole business
bloodier than most, and noisier.
I thought the palace floor
would run with blood.
How can the slaves be spared death,
when they know such secrets?
How can she let her monstrous offspring live?

Nobody sees or hears me
slipping among the mess,
stealing the umbilicus.
Something will always
bind me to my half-brother.

Pasiphaë Meets Her Youngest Child

Not my baby. Never mine, though it stank out my womb
and tore me open, getting born. I thought that I would die.

It was Minos who defied the god, not I.
I'm simply the vessel where the poison was poured.

I'm sick to think of how I fell under that spell
and cannot bear to think of what I did.

The mess this thing made goring out of me
means I will never dance that way again.

I ought to kill the wretched calf. I can't.
I daren't. I fear it is the offspring of a God.

I'll bind my breasts to stop the flow of milk and bind
my heart against a mother's love.

I see how Ariadne's looking down on me.
I'll punish her. I still have power. I'll have her fear me still.

I'll order her precious girls to be the nursemaids of the monster –
to follow the beast into the labyrinth.

Section Three

Into The Labyrinth

The Dark Stink-Song of the Labyrinth

We are the people who will sing this song
dark stink-song of the labyrinth

The Mazemaker's Daughters
We will go first, who all our lives went last.
The daughters of the great inventor, Daedalus.
Slave-girls, disposable, thrown into the maze like trash.

Pasiphaë
I'm Pasiphaë, great Queen of Crete.
Once I ruled as equal with King Minos.
His arrogance brought down the wrath of the Gods.
The curse fell heavily on me
broke me – soul and body.
My husband rules still, arrogance unchecked.
Where is the justice in that judgement?

Ariadne
I'm Ariadne, daughter to King Minos.
Once I was his favourite, destined to rule Crete.
My mother's sluttishness has changed all that.
Now I'm invisible, my power stripped away.
Who'd want to rule the cesspit Crete's become?

The Minotaur
I sing last.
The never-should-have-been.
The terrible wonder of the world –
my roar will shake the whole earth inside out.

The Ladies of the Labyrinth

When the news trembles through the palace –
panic rumours about the birth of a monster-prince –
the court orders the inventor to find a solution.

He cleverly engineers a labyrinth to hold the beast,
builds it with his usual panache for mathematical precision
but we, his daughters, fashion its texture,
weave and stitch its fabric into place.

We drench the maze in subtle shades of dark
make the paths to dead ends more seductive still,
make some walls porous, some dense slab.

Even the Mazemaker himself has no idea of all its secrets,
those suggestions we whispered in his sleep
when the labyrinth was conceived.

Among the corridors of mirrors and baffles
made to amplify howls, magnify the monstrous,
we glide fearless but forgotten,
nameless daughters at the centre of the maze.

Nursemaids of the Minotaur

His bestial suck draws blood,
his response to lullabies a bellow,
but the hammering of his chest
speaks of a fire, hungering perhaps
for language, freedom, gentleness,
the company of others like himself.

How Shall We Mind The Minotaur?

How shall we mind the Minotaur?
Neglect will feed the monster in him.
Shall we madden him with starvation
till he lusts after human flesh? His roar
will turn to ice the blood of any hero.

Shall we soothe the Minotaur?
Lull the man-beast into quietness,
make his imprisonment a harmless dream,
feed him buttercups and grass
till he succumbs to bovine stupor?
Tame him, make him impotent.

Shall we master the Minotaur?
Use him as animal, till he forgets his human half.
Break him, leap on his back as shrieking maenads
goad him to gallop from the maze?
We will bring terror everywhere and lay the world to waste.

Dare we love the Minotaur?
Give him his birthright,
let him find the natural grace
harnessed to his strength,
permit him to be a kind of miracle.

The Minotaur

My first girl   smell meadow
yellow cream   crushed buttercups
suck her   gulp her   bite
till she blooms bruise

smell sour fear-stuff
am different-hungry   am all bull

thrust   grunt   hammer

grunt   hammer   thrust

hammer   thrust   grunt

tear   flesh   open

lick   blood   rub

wetness   howl   utterness

eat her   lungs   liver   limbs

want her
yellow butter   warm fresh
in me
why   cold   still   white
not moving?

Ariadne Enters the Maze

I enter the maze with the sinew in my hand.
It throbs. This solid rock. Is it pulsing?
Who is this hag coming towards me,
her face green, contorted, barring my way
an evil grin splitting her face in two?
It can't be one of my slave-girls.
They've always been too scared of me.

I tell myself I can slip in and out.
I know the spells and know
whose child I am,
what power is mine.
Yet some great stink, some awful trick
within this labyrinth
shuts out this knowledge, screams that I'm a fool.

I haven't met my half-brother yet
but his echoing howls
smash into the core of me.
Hard to hold onto this cord.
It seems to crackle with his pain.

I slip on blood and rotting flesh,
corpses of rats and other vermin,
discarded human bones.
I dare not think of what my brother does.

I will master this.
I must retreat for now.
I will return
to learn the secrets of this pulsing underworld.

The Nameless Ones

We have names.
Secret names we tell nobody.
We're lumped together seen as
the daughters of Daedalus
or Ariadne's shadows
and now we are
the minders of the Minotaur
the ladies of the labyrinth

We are very different –
Chrysoula is not Petaloula.

Black Mirrors of the Minotaur

dark rocks   hurt   burn

      show monster-me   bellow-face

want light rocks   bright

   like in palace

      No want dark rocks

show monster-me   hurt and hurt.

Where light rocks?

      where light rocks show me   miracle-me   magic me

Minos?   What you see in mirror

      in your light palace?

Behind mirror you polish and polish

     is me.

Never far.   I majesty like you.

I more. I magic horned creature.   Double unicorn!

   Any corner in your labyrinth   turn

I'm there

Never far.   I pound   bellow

rage in your dreams   your darkness.

I charge you   Minos.

Know yourself.

Ariadne Curses her Fate

I wouldn't rule this cesspit if you paid me.

I have so little power. I play at it –
giving my father donkey ears, a scratchy scrotum, boils,
making him lust after the hares his lurchers chase.

These itchy little woman-spells are not enough.
I need to wield my full power in a state that's worth my pains.
I must be free of Crete.

I wouldn't rule this cesspit if you paid me.

The Minotaur Rages

Every seven years,

      wolves' howl hollows me.

sniff my freedom   head down

      paw the earth   smell sun

chase its spore

      taste huge blue   deep green.

My father   mighty bull   beyond all others

a thunder god   who will be revenged.

Any corner in my labyrinth.

                Turn

       I'm there

          I'm there

Ariadne Returns to the Maze

Last time I forgot the sword!
This magic sword will cut through all illusion
will light to warn of danger
will always find its target.

This time I enter with sinew and sword.
I cannot fail. This time I've courage,
the spell-bound birth-cord of my brother
beats with my heart beat
slow and steady, steady and slow.
Time to end my brother's misery.

Now I see how the dark walls of the labyrinth
really do pulse as if alive and breathing.
Now I see the way the rocks mirror and distort.
Some of these slabs that seem so solid are quite porous –
others give way as easily as gossamer.
The sword of truth shows me all this.

I see the baffles put in place, disguised so cunningly.
They amplify the monster's roar.
That's why it seems as loud as an earthquake
Thundering from everywhere at once.
I'm sure the victims die of fear before the monster finds them.

This man approaching me is not a man at all,
just one of those toys Daedalus made for me –
an old croaker, his voice box broken.
Why do my slave girls come towards me?
They seem like wraiths and I read in their eyes
a desperate power.

They bow to me, from habit, but I see
insolence in their attitude. I know where the power lies.
It's not with me. My sword's target isn't these poor wretches.

Dionysus Visits the Minotaur in a Dream

You sense your father is a god – you're right!
It's understandable you think it is Poseidon
or Zeus Himself – a great one for bull-aping
especially when impregnating mortals.

No. It was I, Dionysus, who took the bull's form
just at the moment when your mother opened up
eager and wet and willing.
I gave her the time of her life

and in your dreams I'll come to you my boy
teach you dance and song, wine and merriment.
Your daytime life might be a torture,
but at night we'll gallop in meadows
dripping with green and nectared dew.
I'll pour you honey-wine and show you open skies.

Ariadne Foresees the Coming of Theseus

The sword shows me the Minotaur, my half-brother.
I look into his eyes and weep.
He must be released from torment.

Though I came close enough to smell his death
and though the sword burned with knowledge of his death
I see clearly in the blade's reflection –
it is not for me to kill him.

In the sword's blade, a beautiful boy
with the curve of a whip,
the grace and muscles
of one who leaps the bulls.

He is a prince. In his face I see
a kingdom worthy for my rule.
He is a man to love,
a man to wield this sword of power, my father's gift.
He will sever the bull-head from the man.

I'll give him the magic clue –
so many dark and powerful spells
twisted in this thread.
At its core the bloody cord that bound
my brother to my mother –
beast to bitch.

It will lead my hero prince
to the monster he must face
and lead him back again
in triumph, the bull-head in his arms.

We'll all be free.

Section Four

Out of the Labyrinth

Chrysoula And Petaloula
the Mazemaker's Daughters argue

Petaloula
There's a smell! Do you get it? Something different.
This is   familiar   it's our father   and our brother.
How can this be?   What are they doing in the labyrinth?
Daedalus   Icarus   Where are you?

Chrysoula
Why are you shouting out to them? Let them get lost.
Father's bound to think he knows the maze.
He'll never guess the subtle tricks we've added since he built it!
He's always thought himself clever enough
to work his own way out of anything.
Let him just try escaping from this labyrinth!
I'd love to see his face when he realises he can't!
Let's frighten him the way we frightened Ariadne.
Feed him to the Minotaur

Petaloula
Listen to me. Have we turned into monsters?
Our own father. Our own brother.
We need to welcome them, shout out for them.

Chrysoula
Why should we shout for them? I didn't hear them shout for us –
You'd have thought they had no daughters, no sisters.
How dare our father just stand back, say nothing
as we were thrown into his precious labyrinth like trash?
Let him rub his nose in the stink of his invention.
Let him bark his shins and weep for terror.
Don't shout for them! I never heard them shout for us!
You're too soft, sister. Always have been.
             I say: *Feed them to the Minotaur!*

Petaloula
You'll wear yourself out with your cursing.
Forgiveness takes more strength, more courage
than any brutal act of vengefulness and its rewards –

Chrysoula
Stop preaching, lily-livered sister!
I'll never forgive him for burying us alive,
getting us into this mess by building
that obscene contraption for the Queen,
then this vile prison.
Feed him to the Minotaur!
But first I'll scratch their eyes out with my own neglected nails –
torment them like we tortured Ariadne when she first came here –
let the monster's gaping maw appear right in their face!

Petaloula
Stop ranting. Start thinking. Use your brains.
If anyone can find a way out of this vile prison,
it will be Daedalus, the genius, the great inventor.
For our sake, we should let him live.

Chrysoula
Oh yes, of course he'll find a way out!
I suppose he'll make us wings so we'll fly out of here!
In your dreams, sister. Get real!
Deadalus the great inventor is just a prisoner now!

Petaloula
He was always such a favourite with the king.
What has he done that Minos has flung him in here?
Do you think he did shout out for us at last?

continued overleaf

Chrysoula
Hardly. He won't have done anything.
It'll just be a whim of the king's.
Minos has become a crazy tyrant –
all arrogance and cock –
ever since that bull came out of the sea.

Poseidon should have punished Minos – not us.
The God's curse fell hard upon the women.
Broke us all – body and spirit –
leaving the men untouched and arrogant as ever!

The Killing of the Minotaur

Who can say what happened at that murder?
Beheading is a ghastly business
and even a half-bull's neck is thicker than a man's.

However meekly he gave himself to Theseus
he must have thrashed in death-throes,
animal instinct must have taken over
so he gored his murderer.

Some say that as the lifeblood left the beast
Dionysus appeared and cast a spell.
The Minotaur appeared for that moment
utterly magnificent and none could doubt
he had divinity.

Some say – but storytellers will say anything –
that once his head was severed
from the bleeding stump there grew –
like a bud another head – a frightened child's.
Dionysus held the bleeding monster in his arms
and the pair danced their way out of the labyrinth.

On Naxos, in the guise of Dionysus' servant,
the monster learned at last to be his sister's friend,
and learn the complicated dance steps needed
to grow into that complex creature, Man.

Does he dance in the Elysian fields?
Does he weep for prisoners everywhere
even as he feasts on buttercup wine?

Ariadne's Shadows

So Theseus has killed the Minotaur,
holds his horned head in pride.
Ariadne, you've betrayed your brother.
Thus you will be betrayed.

Stench of blood.   Endless ghastly screams.
We move from shadows, from our half-dreams, in a daze.
One crude act has smashed the subtle maze.

More than the Minotaur has been killed.
We shudder at Theseus' boastful shout.
Our hidden magic has been crushed and spoiled.
Violence turns us inside out.

Now the world will be harsh lights and logic
ruled by deadlines and the limits of cold reason
that measures time by neither tide nor season.

Sisters of Icarus

Cocooned so long in Ariadne's silk,
we've dreamed the moment:
the flourish and the letting go,
the swooped dive, the perfect balance
the stretched out feathertipped
deep plummet   rockhurtling fall
that turns
to a smooth floating glide,
a slow upward drift.

Black rocks beg for the shadow of our wings.
The ocean's emerald and amethyst,
the kelp and heather-scented breezes
tempt us to try our green and pale blue wings.

We knew the sun would melt them.
We waited on rocks to let the feeble banners dry.
Can they really hold our weight
and the weight of our poor broken brother?
The only way to find out is to try,
to flex our toes, prepare for flight.

Fly.

Some suggestions for further reading

Birtwistle, Harrison (2008) *Minotaur*
(Libretto by David Harsent). Boosey & Hawkes, London

Bleakley, Alan (1984) *Fruits of the Moon Tree:
The Medicine Wheel & Transpersonal Psychology.*
Gateway Books, London

Cottrell, Leonard (1969) *The Bull of Minos.*
Macmillan, London

Fagles, Robert (1998) trans. *Homer: The Iliad.*
Penguin Classics, London

Graves, Robert (1955). *The Greek Myths:* 2 volumes.
Revised 1960. Penguin, Harmondsworth

MacGillivray, J Alexander (2000) *Minotaur: Sir Arthur
Evans and the Archaeology of the Minoan Myth.*
Hill & Wang, New York

Pendlebury, John D (1939) *The Archaeology of Crete:
an introduction.* Methuen, London

Renault, Mary (1962) *The Bull from the Sea.*
Longman, London

Oversteps Books Ltd

The Oversteps list includes books by the following poets:

David Grubb, Giles Goodland, Alex Smith, Will Daunt, Patricia Bishop, Christopher Cook, Jan Farquarson, Charles Hadfield, Mandy Pannett, Doris Hulme, James Cole, Helen Kitson, Bill Headdon, Avril Bruton, Marianne Larsen, Anne Lewis-Smith, Mary Maher, Genista Lewes, Miriam Darlington, Anne Born, Glen Phillips, Rebecca Gethin, W H Petty, Melanie Penycate, Andrew Nightingale, Caroline Carver, John Stuart, Rose Cook, Jenny Hope, Hilary Elfick, Anne Stewart, Oz Hardwick, Angela Stoner, Terry Gifford, Michael Swan, Maggie Butt, Anthony Watts, Joan McGavin, Robert Stein, Graham High, Ross Cogan, Ann Kelley, A C Clarke, Diane Tang, Susan Taylor, R V Bailey, Alwyn Marriage, Simon Williams, Kathleen Kummer, Jean Atkin, Charles Bennett, Elisabeth Rowe, Marie Marshall, Ken Head, Robert Cole, Cora Greenhill, John Torrance, Michael Bayley, Christopher North, Simon Richey, Lynn Roberts, Sue Davies, Mark Totterdell, Michael Thomas, Ann Segrave, Helen Overell, Rose Flint, Denise Bennett, James Turner, Sue Boyle, Jane Spiro, Jennie Osborne, John Daniel, Janet Loverseed, Wendy Klein and Sally Festing.

For details of all these books, information about Oversteps and up-to-date news, please look at our website and blog:

www.overstepsbooks.com
http://overstepsbooks.wordpress.com

44